I Asked Her Out, She Said Yes -
Now What?

I Asked Her Out, She Said Yes - *Now What?*

A CRASH COURSE IN DATES THAT LEAD TO RELATIONSHIPS

Jarett Waite

Sophic Publishing House
St. George, Utah

ISBN: 978-0-9843540-0-9
Library of Congress Control Number: 2009912232

Published by Sophic Publishing House,
an imprint of Sophic Printing
67 E. St. George Blvd. #10
St. George, Utah, 84770

Cover © 2010 Sophic Printing
Printed in the United States of America

For Jenna

the love of my life

Acknowledgements

I would like to thank everyone who read and critiqued the many drafts of this book. Their suggestions and ideas were invaluable and greatly assisted me in improving my manuscript.

A special thanks goes to Sarah Cypher, my editor. She was great to work with and gave me many excellent recommendations.

Jamieson Greer, Audrey Zohner, Edie Waite, and Jenna Waite were wonderful copy editors. Jenna in particular painstakingly scrutinized all of the advice I give in this book to make sure I was on the right track.

Thank you all so much.

Contents

Chapter 10

I Asked Her Out, She Said Yes - *Now What?*

Chapter 1

WHAT THIS BOOK IS ALL ABOUT

This book is a short, practical guide on how to be truly successful at dating, with an emphasis on what guys can and should do to properly and respectfully treat girls. It covers a variety of subjects including respect, prudence, thoughtfulness, creativity, confidence, being a fun person, and being yourself. It also includes a first date walk-through with step-by-step instructions for a great date. Upon completion of this book, you will have a good idea about what it takes to make a girl feel like a queen and how to cultivate long-lasting relationships.

I would also like to explain from the get-go what this book is not. It is not a guide on how to pick up girls easily. It does not contain magical pick-up lines or mystical methods to trick girls into liking guys. Rather, it's a simple, straightforward, logical guide to dating the right way and making the girl you're interested in feel great about the date.

You may have noticed that this book is short. Rest assured, this is on purpose. I wrote this book to be as approachable as possible. My hope is that you'll be able to get through it in a few sittings, and then tuck it away as a quick reference for the future.

Also, this book has been written from a male perspective and is directed towards guys. Nonetheless, it may prove just as valuable for girls. First, it's a great gift for a boyfriend who needs a little help. Second, it outlines qualities and traits that a girl should look for in a guy that will make relationships stronger and more meaningful. Third, a lot of the advice given in this book isn't necessarily gender-specific. Almost all the principles discussed

2

can be turned around and used to make a guy feel like a million bucks.

I dated for a long time before I met my wife. I started out like most guys – more or less wandering through a dating landscape that I didn't exactly know how to navigate. Dating can be pretty tricky sometimes, and unfortunately there's no universal instruction manual on how to date. Like most people, I made my fair share of mistakes. I tried too hard in some relationships. I was too distant in others. I went after the wrong type of girl a few times. It was quite a challenge trying to figure it all out. Through it all, though, I learned a lot.

After all this trial and error, my dating techniques improved significantly. To my surprise, several of my girlfriends thanked me for being what they called a "good dater." Their compliments seemed a little strange to me, so I didn't really read into them. Soon other girls began probing me to find out why I was good at dating. I didn't know what to tell them, so I had to sit down and really think about what made the way I dated different from most other guys. I came up with a few ideas and jotted them down.

Time went on, girls came and went, and then finally everything came together and I found myself in a meaningful relationship with the girl that would eventually become my wife. At the urging of her and many other people, I decided to write this book to share exactly what I have learned about dating and how girls really want to be treated. No gimmicks, no tricks, just plain old, down-to-earth advice that worked for me and will work for you.

Above all, remember that every relationship is different. Use the principles of this book as guidelines, but pick and choose when it comes to actual application. Find what works best for the situation and run with it. Now let's get to it!

Chapter 2

IT'S ALL ABOUT RESPECT

Successful dating boils down to one thing: respect. If a girl feels that you're approaching her with genuine respect, just about everything else in this book will fall into place. Respect is a firm foundation for any relationship, dating or otherwise. In this book, respect means that you honor a girl and hold her in high regard. It's being considerate and especially attentive to her feelings. It's truly listening to her and being sensitive to her needs. Above all, if you respect a girl, you trust her judgment and allow her to make her own decisions.

Another way to look at respect is that you want to treat your date like a queen. This may sound a little dramatic, but it's her night, and one of your main goals should be to make her feel special. If nothing else comes out of a date, a girl should at least go home happy and feeling good about herself.

In this chapter, we'll break down how to be respectful into two categories: don't be a player and be a nice guy.

Don't Be a Player

Contrary to what some might have you believe, one of girls' top dating priorities is to avoid the players. Accordingly, you don't want to be mistaken for one—and especially don't want to actually be one yourself. Let's start with a definition of what exactly is a player.

A player dates several people at once. Players often pit their dates against one another, using jealousy to start a competition for his or her attention. They think nothing of toying with the emotions of others, or of having physically affectionate relationships with more than one person at a time. To them, a kiss is part of the game—not something special. Rather than seeking a serious, long-lasting relationship, players are always on the lookout for the next best thing. They may have a lot of fun in the short term, but that's just it; everything is short-term for them. With this game plan, players never really settle down and find a satisfying, enduring relationship.

Being a player doesn't sound too great when it's painted in this light, does it? Or even if it does still sound like fun, is this really the type of person that you want girls to peg you for?

Dating should not be a contest for your attention, no matter how much you would like it to be. Don't get me wrong—it's good to have options. You don't want to put all your eggs in one basket until you're sure that you're ready for that bigger commitment. If you're casually dating a few different girls, just be sure to not talk about your "other options" when you're out with one of them. She is the queen for the night and doesn't want to hear about the competition. Also, stay away from physical affection (apart from a hug after a date) until you narrow your options. Just holding hands with a girl can send very strong signals, depending upon the girl, so be careful where you draw the line. You can never be too cautious when you're just starting out.

Players are notorious for teasing. This is part of what makes them successful at dating. Kind, fun teasing is healthy in relationships and can be lots of fun. Just watch out for biting sarcasm or saying anything that could be construed as mean or rude. Don't joke about her looks, her weight, her family, her job, or any other personal part of her life. Keep the teasing friendly. If you're not sure how she'll react to your next crack, then just keep it to yourself.

Be a Nice Guy

Many guys are convinced that "nice guys" only get stomped on in the dating world; that girls only want to date jerks who treat them like dirt. In some ways, unfortunately, they're right. All too often girls don't give nice guys half a chance as they actively pursue jerks that don't deserve their attention. Just accept this as a fact of life. However (and thankfully), not all girls think this way. In fact, a majority of girls think just the opposite. Many girls who gravitate towards jerks and players eventually realize with time and maturity that they are a waste of time.

Look at the big picture. Are you really going to be happy if your relationship is based on being a player, or rude, or selfish? Do you really want to be a jerk anyway? I'm not saying that you need to be a wimp or a pushover—just don't be mean or cocky. Jerks tend to be very confident, which may explain why girls so often go after them. Your goal is to be a *confident nice guy*. You'll be much happier in the long run, as will your future spouse. "Easier said than done," I hear you saying. Don't worry, we'll discuss confidence in Chapter 6.

So what does it take to be a nice guy? Here are a few of the mandatory things:

- Open doors to cars, buildings, etc.
- Be kind and gentle
- Have good manners
- Be attentive to her needs
- Give genuine compliments
- Plan dates with her comfort in mind
- Avoid putting others down around her

Something that also merits your consideration is the simple act of not walking in front of a girl whenever possible. When you pick her up for a date, allow her to walk out the door before you. You may need to direct her towards your car, but let her walk beside you or in front of you. This is a very small way of demonstrating that she's just as important as you are.

You never, ever want your date to feel uncomfortable or self-conscious. This may seem like common sense, but men sometimes just don't notice the little things that can really sour a date. One simple example is not letting a girl know how she should dress for a date. Guys often make the mistake of planning a surprise date and keeping it so secretive (on purpose or inadvertently) that the girl has to guess about what she should wear. All too often, the end result is that she dresses inappropriately and feels out of place.

If you're going someplace nice, be sure to let her know that she needs to dress up. If you're doing something informal, you certainly don't want her to show up in her prom dress, so let her know that casual dress is fine. If you're going outside and it might be cold, don't miss the boat and forget to tell her to dress warmly. Her comfort is one of your top priorities.

Let's be honest, you'll probably get stomped on a few times in your dating life if you're a nice guy. You'll most likely go through a few relationships until you find a girl that truly appreciates your kindness. It's worth the wait, trust me. Too much of dating and hanging out is superficial. Finding a "nice girl" will be both refreshing and comforting. Just hang in there.

Chapter 3

BE

PRUDENT

Think about the type of girl you are looking for. Is she grounded and in control of her life? Is she wise? Does she practice good judgment in everything she does? Does she think through her actions ahead of time? If so, you're looking for a girl that's prudent.

Girls ask themselves the same questions as they consider whether or not they'd like to date you. Invariably, prudence will set you apart from the crowd. In this chapter we'll discuss three different ways of using prudence in dating: have your head on straight, read signs correctly, and practice moderation.

Have Your Head on Straight

What does "have your head on straight" mean? It's very simple. You don't do or say dumb things. You consider how your actions will affect others and plan accordingly. You have firm goals and are always working towards them. You don't loose your temper. When you have your head on straight, you treat others well and deal with them fairly.

Aren't girls always saying guys are way too immature? Well, this is a piece of the puzzle. Thinking through your actions will help you become a more understanding and empathetic person—two qualities that make for a more mature individual.

Even for a simple date, you should plan ahead and think of the different reactions your date might have to whatever you will be doing. For instance, say you drag her to your favorite restaurant or hangout for three hours where you can't hear each other talk. Even if she didn't mind starting the evening out there, a considerate guy will stay alert for cues that the noise or atmosphere is bothering her, and have a few quieter, backup options in mind.

Having your head on straight also means that you watch what you say and how you say it. Most girls are sensitive to word choice and tone of voice—not just in arguments or stressful situations, but especially in the information-gathering environment of a first date. Simple statements voiced in the wrong tone can be misconstrued easily, upset others, or reflect poorly on you. For example, a simple statement such as, "Our food is sure taking a long time," can come across as being concerned that you'll miss your movie time or, alternatively, that you're really annoyed with your waiter.

One more thing for you to consider is the way you act around your family and friends *will* eventually seep into your relationships with girls. Girls really do pay attention to how guys treat their mothers. They also watch how you treat your friends, waiters in restaurants, and even the maintenance guy who comes to fix your apartment toilet. Simply being considerate of others' feelings goes a long way.

I Asked Her Out, She Said Yes - Now What?

Read Signs—Correctly

A common pitfall in dating is the tendency to read signs incorrectly and jump to conclusions. Of course you want to know if she really likes you, if she wants to go out again, or if she wants to kiss you! You need signs. You can find them in a person's behavior, in your conversations with them, from what they tell their friends, and a myriad of other things.

Signs are a vital part of dating and you don't want to be oblivious if a girl is trying to send vibes your way. I've heard many girls say, "Can't he take a hint?" both when a girl was interested and when she was trying to ditch the guy. The trick is to not read too far into any one sign, lest you misinterpret it. Unfortunately, we all tend to give too much weight to one or two signs when our hearts are on the line—and to make matters worse, girls and guys send and interpret signals in different ways. To put this latter idea to the test, I asked several people what kind of signs they use and what they mean. The results of my findings are in the tables that follow.

Sign: Smiling	
Male Meaning	Female Meaning
• I like you • I'm just friendly • You smiled at me, so I smiled back and that's all	• I like you • I'm friendly and smile at everyone • I want to give you my number

Sign: Sending a Text Message	
Male Meaning	Female Meaning
• I like you • I'm lonely • I'm checking to see if you like me • It doesn't mean anything	• I like you • I'm very friendly • I'm bored • I'm shy, but still trying to show interest in you

Sign: Asking to Study Together	
Male Meaning	Female Meaning
• I'm looking for a way to hang out • I'm trying to find an easy way to pass a class	• I like you • I really need help and you're the smartest person I know

Sign: Stopping by Randomly	
Male Meaning	Female Meaning
• I like you • I'm going after your roommate • Watch out, I'm probably a stalker	• I like you • You have a cute roommate • I'm bored and your door was open

Sign: Making Cookies	
Male Meaning	Female Meaning
• I like you a lot, so I'm trying really, really hard • I wanted to do something original and nice for you	• You seem nice and I'd like to get to know you better • The way to a guy's heart is through his stomach

Sign: Talking/Flirting	
Male Meaning	Female Meaning
• I like you • I'm really friendly • Talking to you will help me meet your roommate	• I like you • I'm just a flirt • I can't tell when I'm being friendly vs. flirting

Sign: Avoiding Someone	
Male Meaning	Female Meaning
• You scare me • I'm just too busy to be interested in you right now • I like you a lot and don't know what to do	• It doesn't mean anything • I'm just really busy right now • I don't want to go out with you • I'm shy

Do you see how difficult it is to interpret signs? It's amazing how many different ways people can read and send signals. So what should you do about signs?

First, you look for obvious signs. If a girl is avoiding you like the plague or is somehow always too busy to spend time with you, take this series of signs in stride and move on. Second, avoid the temptation to look for signs in everything. Take note of how she acts around you, but don't watch her every move for an indication of whether or not she's interested. You'll drive yourself crazy, and probably over-interpret a "sign" that is really nothing at all. Third, avoid reading too far into the signs that you do see. Take them at face value and keep going. Some girls are oblivious to the fact that they're even sending signals.

Finally, don't jump to conclusions! Look for a series of signs that direct you one way or another before you make any big decisions. The trick is to be prudent when interpreting signals. Are you starting to see the importance of prudence?

Practice Moderation

Some guys have trouble exercising moderation in doing nice things for girls. I fell into this category at one point in my life. I would get a million ideas for nice things to do for a girl and then I was off to the races. The real danger with this mentality is that too much too soon will scare a girl off.

In one particular relationship, I showered my girlfriend with gifts, flowers, and thoughtful notes. Several times a week I had a surprise for her. This went on for a few months and she seemed very happy with all of the attention.

Everything came crashing down one day when I spent quite a bit of money on concert tickets to see her favorite band. She accepted the tickets, but later called me and told me she felt bad, like she was taking advantage of me. She ended up returning the tickets and breaking up with me. I had done too much.

You certainly want to take care of the girl you're dating, but you have to take it easy and be calm when it comes to pampering her. Too much too soon can set unrealistic expectations for what your relationship will be like in the future. You don't want to set the bar too high.

Moderation also applies to spending money. It is a lot of fun to really go out on the town every once in a while, but that's the key—every once in a while. I know many girls who eventually felt guilty because their boyfriends spent so much money dating them. Spending too much puts undue pressure on a girl to return your kindness.

It's difficult, I know, especially when you're with someone you really like. It's natural to want to do nice things for the girl of your dreams. You just have to keep it under control. Look for 2-for-1 coupons to events and activities, inexpensive but nice restaurants, free concerts, etc. Not all your dates have to be inexpensive (you don't want to appear cheap), but be prudent when planning dates.

One last note, if you want to give her a gift, try to make her something. Rely on the Internet for ideas if nothing comes to mind. Your thoughtfulness will be greatly appreciated and will go a long way.

Chapter 4

DETAILS, DETAILS, DETAILS

Pay attention to the details, *all of them*. All too often guys either don't pay attention to or simply forget the little details that girls share about themselves. It's easy to do—you're focusing on where you're headed next, if you smell okay, if you're talking too much, etc., and not really focusing on what your date is telling you. Forgetting details usually isn't intentional, but with just a little effort, there's no reason why you can't be the exception to the rule and really impress your date.

It all starts with listening. You should pay close attention to everything a girl tells you and take mental notes. Learn the names of her family members. Remember what her favorite foods are. Pay attention to the colors that she wears. Try to find out her hobbies and passions. Always, always get the details.

Speaking of passions, if you have even the remotest interest in something that she's passionate about, make the effort to learn about it so you can have intelligent and interesting conversations with her on the topic—or at least ask intelligent questions about it. Maybe you'll pick up a fun new hobby in the process, and you'll be all the more attractive to her. You don't want to mold your life to hers or show false interest, but if you really like someone, you should at least make an effort to understand what they live for, and why.

Like I stated earlier, forgetting what a girl tells you on a date usually isn't intentional. There's a reason teachers require students to take notes, and the same reasoning applies here. List-making is your friend. Take mental notes when you're with your date; when you get home, write down all the things that she likes and dislikes. This list will prove to be especially helpful when you're brainstorming for date ideas or nice things to do for her. So many times I was strapped for date ideas only to look at my list and realize that the girl I was dating loved something that I had totally forgotten about (which led to a great date).

The rest of this chapter will be devoted to the "small stuff" and being genuine.

The Small Stuff

The "small stuff" really does add up. You should also pay close attention to small, seemingly insignificant things. Girls notice these little details and you'll come across as very thoughtful when you recall one of them.

An example my wife remembers from when we were dating was my effort to make sure that the air conditioning vents were correctly positioned so she would feel comfortable when we drove somewhere. Sure, I could have let her adjust the vents herself, but my concern for such a little thing showed her that I was looking out for her and truly cared.

It's important to note that small acts of kindness often mean much more than large productions or amazing dates. You don't want to look like you're trying too hard. Sometimes the less of a production it appears to be, the better.

One small thing that's easy and effective is leaving notes here and there—on her car, in a book she's reading, on her door, on her fridge, or wherever else she might see a note. Also, don't underestimate the effectiveness of greeting cards. Not only do you get to tell her a thoughtful message without too much effort on your part, but it also shows that you took the time to find a card just for her.

Another staple is flowers—a single stem on her car, a spring bouquet on her doorstep, daisies, tulips, or roses in any other color than red, unless you're in a serious relationship. Stop by your local grocery store for inexpensive flower bouquets (under $15). There is a place for florists and fancy bouquets at some point, but inexpensive flowers generally last much longer than roses or exotic flowers anyway. As with everything else, though, be prudent with your flower-giving; here and there is best. Overkill lessens their effect. I once knew a girl who received so many flowers from a guy that she eventually started putting them down her garbage disposal. Needless to say, the relationship didn't work out.

Most girls have a general sense for what each color means when it comes to flowers, so choose wisely.

- Red—passion
- White—purity or uniqueness
- Yellow—friendship
- Lavender—falling in love
- Pink—"thank you" or happiness
- Orange—enthusiasm or fun

Here are a few other examples of "small things" you can do for a girl:

- In the winter, scrape her car windows early one morning.
- Take out her garbage.
- Drop by unexpectedly to say hello and see if you can help her with anything.
- Take lunch to her at work.
- Find an easy fudge recipe and make it for her. Drop it off on a lazy Sunday.
- Send her a text message complimenting her on something.

- Make cookies or brownies for her.
- Rent her favorite movie (even if it's not exactly your favorite). Do some research on the background of the movie online for some easy and interesting conversation.
- Help her make dinner without being asked.
- Clean up after dinner without expecting praise.
- Buy her favorite candy bar and give it to her at an unexpected time.
- Find a poster or some knick-knack related to something she loves and give it to her.

Being thoughtful makes all the difference in the world in how a girl feels when she's with you. If you want to make her feel like a queen, drop a single flower by her work that just so happens to be her favorite flower and even her favorite color. You'll score points with the girl and her coworkers (always a plus).

One last note—make sure that you find a girl that reciprocates your thoughtfulness. Balance in relationships is important. If you're the only one making an effort to be thoughtful, someone in the relationship will eventually become unhappy.

Be Genuine

This chapter talks a lot about what to do for the girl you're pursuing. But there's a final caveat. Sometimes, it's not just what you do; it's how you do it.

Most girls can see right through you. They're perceptive and will know if your heart isn't in what you do. So, for instance, always make sure that any compliments you give are sincere. If you can't think of anything sincere, just wait until you do to give the compliment. The same goes for special treats and surprises. There doesn't have to be a heart-felt reason behind everything you do, but make sure you're doing things for the right reasons.

If you are genuine, then your intentions are good and you are able to stand behind your actions. You try hard to always be honest. You are sincere, open, and real. When you do something nice for a girl, you do it to brighten her day, not just to receive praise. You're truthful in all of your conversations—so don't blow things out of proportion, exaggerate, or make things up. Sooner or later girls will find out the truth, and then you'll just look dumb or dishonest.

Chapter 5

CREATIVITY COUNTS

D ating can be very boring. For the majority of girls, it's like watching the same movie over and over, only with different actors. What makes it worse is that there's a multiplier effect. You take a girl out to dinner and a movie, then the next weekend someone else does the exact same thing. The following weekend she goes out and sees a movie with someone else. It's the same date over and over, and the time you took her out just blends in with her other dates.

Don't get caught in this cycle and be classified as "any other guy." You're way better than that. Creative dating will excite the girl you're interested in and keep you in her mind long after the date.

Let's be honest, not everyone is creative. That's okay. Some people are creative and just don't realize it. Regardless, dating is so much more fun when the guy goes out on a limb and is creative. Most of the time, it doesn't take much. It's simply looking for ways to catch a girl off-guard. Day to day activities can always be spiced up a little, and putting a spin on normal, standard dates makes them much more exciting and memorable.

In this chapter, we'll first discuss what I mean by the phrase "catching a girl off-guard" and then we'll discuss creative dating.

Catching a Girl Off-guard

Almost all girls love surprises. They love spontaneity. Life can become pretty hum-drum, so when you can mix it up a bit, you're sure to catch her attention. I'm not talking about running away to Mexico or anything crazy like that. Rather, small things can really set you apart from the crowd. Details, details, details...remember?

If you haven't read through the previous chapter, here are a few ideas to help you get in the mindset of catching a girl off-guard:

- Give her flowers for no particular reason when she's not expecting them.
- Place a nice note in a random place at a random time.
- Be crafty and make her a homemade card.
- Make her favorite dinner without her knowing about it.

Do you get the gist of what I'm talking about? Surprise her, for heaven's sake!

While most girls enjoy surprises, as with everything else, don't forget to be prudent. You want to appear grounded and in control of your life, but if you're always doing something off-the-wall, you may scare her away. Also, some girls don't like surprises, so you should probably start with something small to see how she reacts and then go from there.

One last thing, catching a girl off-guard on an off-day may not be a good idea. In other words, if a girl is having a bad day, the last thing she may want is an unexpected event. On the other hand, you could potentially turn her day around by surprising her with something nice (like a flower or note), so feel out each situation carefully before you dive in.

Putting a Spin on Standard Dates

You may be thinking right now that dinner and a movie is the worst date ever because of the multiplier effect explained in the beginning of this chapter. Dinner and a movie is actually fine, but why not make it a theme night? Go to a sixties diner and then watch a movie set in that time period. Stop by a thrift store after dinner and dress up in clothes that match the theme of the movie you're going to watch. Watch a movie in 3D. The goal is to stand out in her mind and demonstrate that you're different from other guys.

My wife fondly recalls our first date that I dubbed "Little Italy" night. After a nice but simple homemade Italian dinner, we watched *Il Postino* (a subtitled Italian movie) on a projector in my apartment. This date wasn't anything too special, but it was definitely out of the ordinary. My wife had actually been on another date that day before ours, but the other guy didn't get a second date. I did because I stuck out from the crowd.

You don't have to morph the entire date, just a part of it. You might start dinner with desert and then work your way backwards, or possibly have a picnic in your living room. Sometimes one small change can make a date much more fun and memorable.

Have you ever had a girl over for breakfast? Even better, have you ever eaten cereal and watched Saturday morning cartoons on a date? Find some of the cartoons from when you were kids on video or DVD and prepare for a blast from the past and a good time. Lunch dates are not very common, either, but a lot of fun. As an added bonus, lunch dates are less formal, almost always less expensive, and usually shorter than other dates. They take a lot of the pressure off of you to entertain her and maintain good conversation for a long time.

When you show up at a girl's door with something really fun planned, she'll recognize how much thought went into the date and appreciate your gesture. In all reality, putting together a fun date demonstrates that you care for the girl you've asked out and want her to feel special. It's a way of saying, "This date is important enough to me to plan an activity I know we'll both enjoy."

I have compiled a small list of additional creative dates that I have tried or would be willing to attempt. It's too long to list here, so check out Appendix A in the back of this book. Dating can be very fun when you decide to not be "any other guy."

Chapter 6

CONFIDENT, NOT COCKY

C onfidence may be the most attractive characteristic a girl can find in a guy. Read that
sentence again, because it's true. That's
right, confidence can really make a big difference
in how girls perceive you. Have you ever wondered
why guys who are arrogant or cocky always seem
to get the girls? One word: confidence.

Confidence is being sure of yourself. It's
knowing where you're going and how you're going
to get there. It's being decisive. It's having control

of your surroundings and not worrying too much about the things that are out of your control. Girls want guys that are leaders.

Be a Leader

Girls are naturally attracted to guys who tread their own path. They want to be with someone that's in charge. They want to be protected, and the most sensible way to do this is to find a guy that can take care of himself and others—a leader. Keep in mind that you don't always have to take the lead, but you don't want to sit in the background all the time, either. Girls don't usually want to date slackers.

So what does it take to be a leader? The first characteristic is decisiveness. When you're put on the spot, you should be able to act quickly without questioning yourself. This easily translates to dating. When you walk into a restaurant, it's nice to ask the girl where she wants to sit, but if she doesn't care or doesn't know, you have to make a quick decision and head that way. How would it look if you sat there contemplating where to sit for a little while? It makes you look unsure of yourself.

After you've made a decision, try to not second-guess it. In the example of choosing where to sit, once you've made a decision, you have to ignore whatever doubts may develop in your mind, such as, "What if she hates this spot?" Just go with it.

Now, if she really does hate the spot, a good leader will also be empathetic and figure out what it will take to make her happy. In this case, ask her where she would be most comfortable. Empathy is putting yourself into someone else's shoes to better understand where they're coming from. When leaders better understand why people act the way they do, it's much easier to make decisions that will keep everyone happier. If you know ahead of time that the girl you're dating doesn't like small spaces, then you'll naturally choose a spot that's open and airy.

Another characteristic of good leaders is a subtle inner faith that whatever decision you make, it'll work out just fine. And if it doesn't work out perfectly, you'll at least figure out a way to fix it. When everything is said and done, you'll be in great shape, as well as everyone involved in your decision. You have to believe in yourself.

There are volumes and volumes of books already written on leadership, so I won't belabor the point. Just remember to be decisive, believe in yourself and your decisions, and be empathetic. This will get you on the right track. Remember that not everyone is born with confidence. If you fall into this category, just be patient and work at it. The more you apply the principles covered in this book, the more success you'll have in dating. Your dates will go smoother, and you'll become more confident in your interactions with girls. It will come; just hang in there.

Don't Be Cocky

Cockiness attracts some girls like crazy, but it's only because cockiness is basically confidence twisted a little and taken too far. Cockiness is best defined as feeling very sure of yourself, and then letting everyone know about it. It's boasting about how great you are and looking down on others.

There's a big difference between being confident and being cocky. An example would be if you were talking about something that you're good at.

Let's say your hidden talent is that you're a great handyman. A confident person might talk casually about some of the things he has fixed when asked, and wouldn't automatically divulge how amazing his work was unless the girl asked additional questions. A cocky person, on the other hand, would brag about how good they were from the get go, and then go on and on about it, whether the girl wanted to hear about it or not.

Cockiness goes right along with the word "jerk," which is exactly what you don't want to be. Remember, the goal of this book is to encourage your inner nice guy and help you win a girl's heart. Cockiness will only get in the way.

Be Humble

You may be asking yourself, "Why is he talking about humility in the chapter about confidence?" The fact of the matter is, really good leaders are just as humble as they are confident. Being humble means that you are aware of your faults. It means that you realize your imperfections. Humility doesn't mean that you should dwell on your faults—simply recognize that you have things to work on. Please don't put yourself down around others. You don't need people feeling sorry for you.

Confidence mixed with humility, while seemingly contradictory, impresses most girls. In fact, being humble about your strengths and accomplishments only makes you look more confident. You don't have to flaunt your strengths to be strong. You demonstrate your strength and confidence by your quiet actions, not by what you brag about to others.

Chapter 7

HAVE FUN

Please, please don't be a dud when you date. You have virtually no chance of another date if you can't loosen up and be engaging. Engaging means flirting without being obnoxious, asking good questions, and volunteering low-key information about your life that will help the girl get to know what your personality is like and what your interests are. It's a lot easier than it seems, trust me—it only means that you enjoy yourself, and let it show. Imagine how you act around your friends when you're in a good mood; there aren't any awkward silences, are there?

We'll cover several topics in this chapter, including how to prepare for a date, how to ask good questions, and how to make your date laugh.

Prepare Well for the Date

The first step is to get lots of sleep the night before the date. You don't want to be nodding off in the middle of dinner or during the movie afterwards. Plus, you need to be running on all gears if you really want to show your best self. Next, review your plans so that everything will go smoothly. Double-check any reservations that you have made, and make sure that you have whatever tickets you need. Call ahead if you're worried about someplace filling up or running out of tickets. Make backup plans, if you haven't already, just in case something falls through.

I have been on countless dates where something didn't quite work out as I planned, but I was able to seamlessly recover thanks to a backup plan. None of the girls ever realized the change in plans. You certainly don't want to be out on your date, have something fall through, and then look like an idiot as you try to figure out what else will be fun for you both. Plan ahead.

Ask Good, Open-Ended Questions

You really need to make a conscious, concentrated effort to be engaging and entertaining. The key is to ask good, open-ended questions, and lots of them. Not only does this open the way for plenty of healthy conversation, but it also demonstrates to the girl that you're genuinely interested in her and want to learn more about her.

You'll be surprised by how much you'll learn about a girl once she opens up, and she will if she's at least a little bit interested in you. If this goes right, you'll both be able to make a much more informed decision after the date as to whether or not you're still interested in each other. You won't have to rely only on her looks, popularity, signs, or a vague sketch of her biography to decide if you're compatible. Why would you want to take out an attractive but boring girl, anyway?

Here are some examples of good, open-ended questions:

- "Where are you from? What's it like there? Did you enjoy growing up there?"
- "Would you want to live there again? Any particular reason why/why not?"
- "Are you going to school right now? What are you studying and why did you choose it as your major?"
- "What do you plan on doing with your major after you graduate?"
- "Do you work? What do you do there? Do you like it? Where else have you worked in the past?"
- "What do you like to do? When did you start _____?"
- "Do you play any sports?"
- "Do you watch any sports or have a favorite sports team?"
- "Do you play any instruments?"
- "Have you traveled much? What's the most interesting place you've been to? Where else would you like to visit?"
- "What do your parents do for a living?"

- "What kind of music do you listen to?"
- "What kind of music do you not like?"
- "Who's your favorite band? Have you ever been to one of their concerts?"

All these questions lend themselves to follow-up questions and engaging conversation. You'll probably want to reword them a little to suit your needs, but you get the idea. Notice that many of the questions inquired about what really makes the girl tick—her interests and passions. That's what you want to find out. Hopefully you'll be just as interested in the same things as she is. Then you're in luck.

If you're nervous about the date, I would recommend that you make yourself a little cheat-sheet with several questions written down that you know you'd like to ask. Keep it in your pocket or somewhere convenient so that you can fall back on it if your mind goes blank. Make sure that if you do need to take a look at it, do it inconspicuously.

The flip side to this section is that you had better be ready to answer any of her questions, and think through how you would respond to your own questions.

Make Her Laugh

Everyone loves to laugh and everyone loves a comedian. Getting a girl to laugh will lighten the mood and make you much more attractive in her mind. She will enjoy spending time with you. Unfortunately, not everyone is born a funny man. Here's where preparation and perhaps even the cheat-sheet come into play again.

Find some good jokes online or wherever and write them down. You don't have to have her rolling on the ground the whole date. Just have a few jokes cocked and ready for a slow moment or when you can't think of something to say or ask.

By all means, if you are the type of person that can be spontaneously funny, use it to your full advantage. "Spontaneous funny" is almost always funnier than "planned funny." Potentially awkward situations occur in many dates, but if you can exploit them as funny moments, you'll avoid possible embarrassment and make the date all the more memorable.

For example, if you're at dinner and finish eating well before she does, say something like, "I guess pretending to study all day long made me hungry!" or "Just my 'starving student' instincts kicking in." If you're not comfortable being funny on the spot, don't worry. Once you've been dating a girl for a while, it becomes much easier.

Jokes made at your own expense are an easy way to maintain informality and show some humility. You'll show your date that you don't take yourself too seriously. Of course, don't make fun of yourself too much—you don't want your date worrying about an underlying self-esteem problem.

Another way to make her laugh is a little kind-hearted teasing. If you're miniature golfing, taunt her a little. A little trash-talk can be fun whenever you're doing something competitive; just make sure to keep it minimal, and if she doesn't reciprocate, drop it. Avoid taboo subjects, too—her looks, her weight, her family, or any other touchy part of her life. Keep the mood light, get her to laugh, and you'll be on track for another date.

A few last warnings: when you're joking around, stay away from anything racist, sexist, or even remotely offensive. Your date may like those kinds of jokes, but chances are she'll be turned off and won't be calling you back. Also, slapstick comedy is appreciated by some girls, but not all. Lastly, don't try too hard to be funny. If your date isn't getting your jokes, roll with the punches and try a different angle. There's nothing worse than a funny man with nobody laughing at him.

Chapter 8

BE
YOURSELF!

Sometimes "being yourself" can be much harder than it sounds. We've all been there— you're on a date with the girl you've been chasing for a while, you're a little nervous, and the pressure is on for you to perform. You don't want to do anything dorky, and you definitely want to impress her somehow. You're considering telling her about your day, but nothing too exciting happened. So what do you do? This chapter will point you in the right direction. We'll first discuss quirks, then we'll go over what to do if you don't consider yourself an interesting person, and then we'll finish up with the end goal of dating.

Quirks

Don't be afraid to talk about your quirks. You know, the stuff that makes you strange—umm—I mean, unique. Let's face it, everyone is weird. I can only think of a few completely "normal" people who I've met in my life, and frankly, they were boring. It's our oddities that make us unique, interesting, and fun. Don't parade around showing off your quirks on a date, but if one comes up, don't shy away from talking about it. She might even have a similar oddity.

It's okay if you really like Star Wars, if you're not a fan of blue M&M's, or if you enjoy making paper airplanes. It's also just fine if you prefer even numbers over odd ones, if clowns freak you out, or if you love karaoke. At worst, the girl you eventually spend the rest of your life with will tolerate your quirks. Ideally, though, she'll think your quirks make you more interesting and attractive.

As an example, I've always been a fan of shopping thrift stores—you just never know what you'll find. After we had been dating for a while, I dragged my girlfriend (who is now my wife) to a thrift shop. She really didn't want to go. With a little coaxing, she started browsing and ended up finding something she liked. The next time we went she wasn't quite as reluctant. Now my wife loves going more than I do. In this case, she actually embraced one of my quirks.

What If I'm Not Interesting?

First off, everyone is interesting in one way or another. That's what the last section was all about. If you feel that you're not very interesting, you may need to change a few things up in your life. Life can get pretty monotonous, filled with things like work, classes, going to the gym, and studying. Even if you do have an interesting job, or an intriguing class, you can really boost your dating resume if you break out of your routine every once in a while. Go out on a limb and try something you have wanted to do for a long time. Find a new hobby. Take an art class, join a soccer team, go see a play, or run a marathon. The sky is the limit.

I also recommend learning about things you want your ideal mate to be interested in. For example, if you would like to date a girl that's a mountain climber, you had better be one yourself. If you're interested in girls that are artistic, find a way to be artistic yourself. The Internet is an amazing thing. You can learn just about anything from experts and novices alike online: I have learned things ranging from cooking to vacuum molding to soldering. Also, don't forget the library. Books are an excellent resource for developing new talents. Plus, you can casually mention your visit to the library on your date. It will make you look intelligent, and if she's into reading, her eyes will light up.

A word of caution: whatever you do, don't sit around and play video games all day. I can safely say that the majority of girls loathe video games, while a few tolerate them. An even smaller minority actually play them. Video games aren't a bad thing, they just shouldn't take up most of your time, and they certainly shouldn't ever be brought up during a date conversation. This is a sure way to send up all kinds of red flags in your date's mind. Get out of the house! It's pretty difficult to talk about your day when you haven't done much.

If you've got free time and really want to score some bonus points with the opposite sex, find a way to serve the community. You don't have to be Ghandi or anything, just take an hour or two every week to do something selfless. There are many commendable community organizations that are always looking for volunteers.

What's the End Goal?

What is the real end goal of dating? I hope that for you, it's to find someone to spend the rest of your life with. So it only makes sense that you should be your true self around the girl who's caught your eye. Why put up a false image when you know that it will eventually crumble? Of course you want to show your best side—a fun, polite, "on" version of yourself; you just don't want to give her false impressions.

Remember that you're looking for someone that compliments you, has fun with you, and understands you. You won't be able to do this if you're not your true self around your date.

Sometimes dating turns into a search for a relationship, any relationship, and at that point it can become pretty tempting to start projecting a different image of yourself. You may act more interested than you really are in the hobbies of the girl you're dating, or you may give up activities you really love just to please her.

If something you love to do is destructive or a waste of time, letting it go might actually be a good thing. But most of the time this isn't the case. A lot depends on your motivation. Hopefully you're always striving to improve yourself, but changing yourself just for the sake of being more attractive to a particular girl usually doesn't end well. You won't be happy in the long run.

Say you love hunting—you've been hunting since you were a kid and look forward to the hunting season every year. Then one day the girl you're dating tells you she thinks hunting is wrong. It will probably be pretty difficult to find a middle ground there. You'll have to seriously weigh the pros and cons of changing to please her, and then go with what's best for the both of you. She might change her position if she really values your relationship. Again, make sure you don't drop activities you love solely to appease a girl.

It's important to always remember that if you present yourself as you really are and a girl loses interest, then she just wasn't the one for you. Coming to terms with this fact can make dating a whole lot easier on your heart. It's one thing to have a mistake you made in a relationship lead to its demise, but if she's just not that into you, it's perfectly acceptable to break up. Most guys end up dating lots of girls until they find the right one, so don't get too hung up when a relationship fizzles.

Chapter 9

DATE WALK-THROUGH

O kay, this walk-through is going to be simple and straightforward. So far, we've talked about what to do and what not to do on a date, so now it's time to put it all together. I'm going to take you through every step of a good date, from start to finish. I have tailored this template to a first date, but almost all of the steps should apply to future dates.

As with everything else in this book, don't feel that you have to follow this guide to the letter.

Choose what will work best for you and then go for it. So here goes:

Step 1

Try to get to know her before you ask her out. Dating is so much easier when you already have a base to work from. Ever wonder why blind dates very rarely turn into anything serious? It's certainly a good idea to already be friends or at least acquaintances before you take her out. Granted, this isn't always possible, so if you've been set up by someone, ask them about the girl so that you can prepare ahead of time with a few questions that might spark some conversation.

Step 2

Ask her out several days in advance. Specifically, you should ask her by Tuesday night for a Friday date and Wednesday for a Saturday date. This serves several purposes. First, it gives you a jump on the competition. It's a real downer when you plan an awesome date only to find out that someone else has already asked her out. Second, if you call too late in the week, she may be embarrassed to admit that she doesn't have plans yet. I know girls that have been asked out the night before the planned date and have made up excuses just to hide the fact that they didn't already have something planned. Third, it's a sign of respect. She shouldn't be rushed into making a decision. Being spontaneous doesn't work well here.

Step 3

When you ask a girl out, don't say, "Do you have anything planned for this weekend?" This is actually one of the absolute worst things that you could ask a girl because it is so ambiguous. It puts the girl in a tight spot because if she says that she's busy, she'll send a negative message, even though she may like you. On the other hand, if she says that she doesn't have anything planned, then she feels that she's sending a "yes" signal, even though she may not be interested at all. It's a catch-22 for the poor girl. I can't count how many times I've heard girls complain about this question. Instead, tell her what you have planned and ask her if she'd like to come. That's all it takes, just a little change to your wording. Be straight forward from the get-go and you'll be good to go.

Step 4

It's almost always better to have everything planned out. If you really want to let a girl down, get in the car and ask, "So, where should we go?" Find out ahead of time what she likes to eat and choose a restaurant accordingly. Plan out each part of the date, and even have a backup plan for anything that might not work out. It also doesn't hurt to plan a few time-fillers just in case you find yourself with a half-hour on your hands. You don't want to act like you're following an itinerary while you're on the date, but having a well-thought-out plan and possibly falling back on a few alternate options without her knowing will make you look more confident and lead to a very smooth date.

Step 5

Wash your car, vacuum it, and make it smell nice. It also doesn't hurt to put some tire shine foam on your tires. This shows her that you made an effort for the date, and girls do notice when you don't clean your car. Even if you drive a clunker or have to borrow a car, still do your best to make it shine. Many girls don't care what kind of vehicle you drive, but they do notice how you take care of it. In their minds, this translates to how well you take care of everything else you own.

Step 6

Pay attention to your clothing and dress appropriately for the occasion. Decide in advance what you are going to wear instead of waiting until the last minute. If you're planning a date where you'll need to dress nicely, be sure to iron your clothes. Wrinkles mean one of two things to a girl—"I'm a slob," or, "This date wasn't important enough for me to spend five minutes to iron my clothes."

Step 7

Show up on time. Punctuality is generally regarded as a good trait and a sign of maturity. If you show up too early, you may appear overly anxious. On the other hand, showing up late sends a signal that you're irresponsible or that you don't care about the date. Plus, showing up late may mess up the time line of your carefully planned date.

Step 8

Walk up to her door and knock or ring the doorbell. Do not stay in your car and honk. That's just plain rude. I'm sure that you don't do this—I'm just checking.

Step 9

When she comes out, compliment her on how she looks. Try to pick out one thing that genuinely impresses you, whether it's her shoes, her shirt, her hair, her purse, or whatever. Make sure that you compliment her early on in the date, probably before you leave her place. Otherwise, you'll forget or it'll be awkward later to bring it up. Make sure that you don't go overboard and give too many compliments. Rather, drop a few well-thought-out compliments and they'll go a long way. Remember: be genuine in your compliments or they'll backfire.

Step 10

Allow her to lead the way (don't walk in front of her). This is a way to show respect.

Step 11

Open her car door. It may seem old-fashioned, but 99 percent of girls want you to open their door for them. It'll show that you're a gentleman. Also, close her door softly. Be gentle.

Step 12

Have good music playing softly in your car. The key words in that last phrase were "good" and "softly." Loud music discourages conversation and may end up giving her a headache. This is a real time to shine if you can find out ahead of time what kind of music she likes. If it's something that you like as well, then this is a prime opportunity to show her that you two have something in common.

Step 13

Ask good questions, and lots of them. See Chapter 7 for more details. Remember to take mental notes of the things you learn about her so you can write them down later.

Step 14

Be yourself and don't be afraid to talk about your life, your friends, and your hopes. Just be sure to not stay on the subject of "you" for too long. Wait to talk about yourself until she asks or until you've talked plenty about her. You're going for confidence and thoughtfulness here, not cockiness.

Step 15

Have fun! Dates are supposed to be fun, right? Be your best self around her and try to get to know her well. Follow your plans and watch for clues as to whether or not she's having a good time. If she's not, adjust your plans.

Step 16

After a great date comes the doorstep scene. Be sure that there is a doorstep scene; i.e., don't stay in your car and drop her off. Thank her for a great time and, if it's appropriate (you honestly feel like there's potential), ask her if she'd like to do something with you again. Lay it out on the line right then and there. You don't need to actually have something planned, just ask her in a genuine tone if she'd like to go out again. Why put up with all of the silly signs (avoiding you, not returning calls, etc.), when she can just tell you right then and there whether or not she's interested. Plus, in this situation you'll be able to assert your interest without being overbearing. Make the question casual and not demanding. Definitely keep in mind that some girls won't want to hurt your feelings and will say yes, but really mean no, so here's a time you should look for signs. Pay attention to how she replies, not just her reply. It shouldn't be too hard to pick up on negative vibes if she's sending any your way.

Step 17

Give her a hug and wish her a good night. That's it! Actually, a hug isn't mandatory and is totally up to you. Most girls see quick hugs as a nice gesture and don't read too much into them. You might feel like it's been a really good date and want to kiss her, but many girls would rather wait until at least the second or third date for a kiss. You don't want to be too forward and scare her off.

Step 18

Okay, so there's one more thing. Don't trip as you walk away, and don't celebrate or sob until you've put a decent amount of space between her doorstep and you.

Quite a list, huh? If you follow these eighteen steps, I assure you that you'll be on track for a great date.

Chapter 10

CLOSING THOUGHTS

As you're looking for girls to date, keep an eye out for girls who display all the characteristics described in this book. Find someone thoughtful, prudent, confident, fun, and not afraid to be herself. These are signs of maturity and will make for a much healthier and fun relationship.

Sure, that other girl may be a hot ticket, but if she isn't empathetic towards others or has no personality, who needs her? Any relationship with a girl who lacks these all-important values is doomed and will drag you down.

Be careful: if a girl doesn't seem to be putting in as much as you are into the relationship, it's a telltale sign that something is wrong. A relationship where one partner does an unequal amount of the work is destined to make someone in the relationship unhappy. I've been in that situation before, trying way too hard to make the girl happy and in the end, she couldn't keep up. I achieved the exact opposite of my goal as she began to feel more and more guilty and unhappy. Prudence and moderation are key elements in successful dating.

So, if you remember one thing from this little book, what should it be? RESPECT. If you respect a girl, you'll want to take care of her the right way and you'll do what I've talked about in this book. In all honesty, girls will think you're amazing if you do just a few of the things that I have suggested. Even more important, the person that you spend the rest of your life with will be forever grateful.

The more tips you try, the better off you'll be, but don't feel like you have to take every word of this book to heart. As I said in the first chapter, every relationship is different. Pick and choose what works best for you and make it your own. Also, be patient with yourself. Many of the tips in this book are character-building and may require time to develop.

When everything is said and done, I sincerely hope you find yourself in an enduring, meaningful relationship. Good luck and happy dating!

Appendix: Creative Date Ideas

Here's a quick reference list of creative date ideas that your date might enjoy:

- Have lunch at a nice café or bistro.

- Eat cereal and watch cartoons on a Saturday morning. Try to find cartoons from when you were kids.

- Take her to a symphony. If you're a student, try to find student tickets. Oftentimes they're 75 percent or more off of the standard ticket price. This means amazing seats for very little money. If you're trying to impress the girl, don't let her know how cheap the seats were. On the other hand, if you're just out for a good time, let her know about the great deal that you found.

- Go to a clean comedy club. This takes a lot of the pressure off of you to make her laugh and is a lot of fun.

- Make dinner together. It's easy, simple, and a great way to get to know each other better. It also demonstrates that you have at least some domestic skills. Be sure to compliment her on the great meal.

- Go to a store and buy your favorite candy. Then go home and make milk shakes with the items.
- Miniature golf is always fun.
- Bumper bowling is off the beaten path of date ideas, but it's a lot of fun. Plus, everyone scores well and the girl doesn't have to worry about being embarrassed by her bowling skills, or lack thereof.
- Go to a Nickelcade. Girls may not generally like video games, but for some reason arcades and ticket-winning games don't fall into the same category in their minds. You may want to stay away from fighting games if you know that she has a problem with them.
- Have an art night. It doesn't matter if you're artistic or not, just have fun with it. Paint with real paint or use watercolor books, whatever you'd like.
- Buy a bag of Laffy Taffy and read the jokes to each other. This is goofy, I admit, but it

works really well for whenever you have to drive for a while.

- Local theatre is almost always a good bet.
- Go to a concert. The local scene is usually a lot of fun and doesn't cost too much. In addition, watch for big-name bands that she'd love to see.
- Sculpt mashed potatoes into wonderful masterpieces.
- Go to a library or bookstore and browse the aisles together.
- Write letters to friends, grandparents, family, etc. This probably wouldn't work as an actual date, but it's a great way to spend time together doing something constructive.
- Rent an old movie. Try to find a movie with Kerry Grant, Jimmy Stewart, or some other classic actor. Check online guides to old movies to find a winner.
- Fly a kite.
- Put together a puzzle.
- Attend community events, fundraisers, or church services together.

- Visit a museum. Do your homework first so that you know what you're talking about.
- Play pool in a good, clean environment.
- Make a mosaic. Go to a thrift store and buy different colored plates, cups, etc. Then go home and break them how ever you want. Make a mosaic out of the pieces. There's a certain refreshing freedom in breaking stuff on purpose.

Notes

Notes

Notes

Notes

About the Author

Jarett Waite was born and raised in a rural community in Idaho. He attended Brigham Young University and graduated with a Bachelors of Science in Business Management in 2005. He met his wife, Jenna, shortly after graduating and they now have two sons, Bryce and Tyler. Jarett owns Laser Mania Family Fun Center in St. George, Utah, and enjoys managing the day-to-day operations. His writing has been featured in trade magazines and he speaks at conventions regularly.

www.ingramcontent.com/pod-product-compliance
Lightning Source LLC
Chambersburg PA
CBHW050548280326
41933CB00011B/1761